Original title:

Harmonious Bends Inside the Wizard Puff

Author: Paula Raudsepp

ISBN HARDBACK: 978-1-80563-406-5

ISBN PAPERBACK: 978-1-80564-927-4

## Mystical Curves of Enchanted Dreams

In shadows dance the silver beams,
A world awash in vibrant schemes.
With whispered winds the starlight gleams,
Carving paths through hidden streams.

Each curve a tale of magic spun,
Where laughter calls and wonders run.
In twilight's grasp, our wishes won,
As day turns soft, and night begun.

# Whispers of the Arcane Mist

Beneath the veil of twilight's glow,
Secrets drift where soft winds blow.
In shrouded woods, the ancients know,
The silent paths where few can go.

The mist unveils a mystic grace,
Each breath a hint, a warm embrace.
Time slips away in this lost place,
Where echoes linger, soft as lace.

## The Melodies in the Twilight Grove

Harmonies weave through branches bare,
As crickets sing in the cool night air.
The wind hums secrets, sweet and rare,
In twilight's arms, we lose our care.

Each note a spell, each chord a bliss,
In nature's heart, we find our reminisce.
With every sound, we gently kiss,
The essence of this magic's tryst.

## Sorcery's Gentle Embrace

In quiet woods where dreams take flight,
Magic dances in soft moonlight.
With every breath, we feel the slight
Of sorcery that feels so right.

A gentle touch within the trees,
The air hums softly, whispers tease.
In nature's grasp, we find our ease,
Where every heart can feel the breeze.

# Enigma of the Floating Veil

In twilight's hush, a ridge appears,
A veil of mist that veils our fears.
It dances lightly, caught in air,
Whispering secrets, hidden, rare.

Beneath its shroud, the world stands still,
Entranced in magic, bending will.
Curious eyes both near and far,
Yearn to unveil what lies ajar.

Each wisp of thought, a thread to weave,
Tales of a night we scarcely breathe.
The veil will lift, or so it seems,
To show what lies beyond our dreams.

With every breeze, it shifts and sways,
Guarded by shadows of bygone days.
Yet in its folds, a promise waits,
Of hidden paths and mystic gates.

So follow close, but heed the call,
Of echoes dancing in the thrall.
For in this realm of soft reprieve,
Awaits the heart that dares believe.

# Chasing the Serpent of Light

In dawn's embrace, a serpent gleams,
A flash of brilliance, sparking dreams.
It weaves through trees with radiant grace,
Leaving a trail of lighted lace.

With every turn, the shadows play,
In sunlight's arms, they dance and sway.
But fearless hearts will not retreat,
For truth awaits where light and shadows meet.

The chase unfolds like ribboned skies,
Where hope takes flight, and courage flies.
Through bramble thorns and whispered sighs,
The serpent leads to faded ties.

Each flicker bright, a fleeting chance,
To grasp the world in daring dance.
And though it twists, and slips away,
The heart beats on, come what may.

So follow fast, the light will guide,
Through misty realms where dreams abide.
In chasing whispers, secrets bright,
You'll find your way, in pure delight.

## Echoes in the Mystic Breeze

When night descends, a quiet sound,
Lingers softly, all around.
With every breath, the whispers flow,
Echoes of tales we long to know.

They swirl like spirits, lost in time,
Treading paths through heart's own rhyme.
Each gentle gust, a phantom sigh,
Calls forth the memories, passing by.

The breeze carries laughter, soft and clear,
A song of longing, drawing near.
It stirs the leaves, ignites the night,
Painting shadows with silver light.

In haunted woods, the secrets weave,
Threads of wishes weaves to believe.
These echoes dance on air so free,
Molding dreams, like waves at sea.

So listen close, when silence falls,
For through the night, the magic calls.
Among the stars, where spirits tease,
You'll find your truth in the mystic breeze.

# The Lullaby of Ancient Shadows

In twilight's cradle, shadows sing,
A lullaby from times of wing.
With tender notes of days gone past,
They weave a spell that holds us fast.

Each whisper soft, a tale of old,
Of secrets shared, and dreams retold.
They lull the heart to sleep so deep,
In arms of night, where mysteries creep.

Beneath the stars, the stories flow,
In gentle streams, like rivers slow.
Though darkness veils what lies ahead,
The shadows guard what must be said.

Dreams flutter wide on whispered wings,
In ancient depths, the silence clings.
And while we drift in cosmic space,
The shadows hum their soft embrace.

So let them guide you through the night,
In shadowed realms, you'll find the light.
For in their song, the truth bestows,
The lullaby of ancient shadows.

# Secrets Carried by the Northern Lights

In twilight's dance, the skies alight,
With secrets spun in colors bright,
A gentle breeze, a whispered tale,
Of ancient dreams that softly sail.

Through emerald fields where shadows play,
The stars join in, a grand ballet,
They twinkle with each heartfelt wish,
A canvas vast, like magic's kiss.

With every pulse, the night transforms,
In waves of glow, the spirit warms,
The northern lights, in silence shout,
Of mysteries that roam about.

Each hue a story, bold, profound,
In nature's grasp, our hearts are bound,
For in the shimmer, we are free,
To share our truths, just you and me.

So look above, as shadows play,
And let the lights show you the way,
For in their glow, we find our spark,
Secrets carried in the dark.

## The Lullaby of Ancient Shadows

In twilight's cradle, shadows sing,
A lullaby from times of wing.
With tender notes of days gone past,
They weave a spell that holds us fast.

Each whisper soft, a tale of old,
Of secrets shared, and dreams retold.
They lull the heart to sleep so deep,
In arms of night, where mysteries creep.

Beneath the stars, the stories flow,
In gentle streams, like rivers slow.
Though darkness veils what lies ahead,
The shadows guard what must be said.

Dreams flutter wide on whispered wings,
In ancient depths, the silence clings.
And while we drift in cosmic space,
The shadows hum their soft embrace.

So let them guide you through the night,
In shadowed realms, you'll find the light.
For in their song, the truth bestows,
The lullaby of ancient shadows.

## Secrets Carried by the Northern Lights

In twilight's dance, the skies alight,
With secrets spun in colors bright,
A gentle breeze, a whispered tale,
Of ancient dreams that softly sail.

Through emerald fields where shadows play,
The stars join in, a grand ballet,
They twinkle with each heartfelt wish,
A canvas vast, like magic's kiss.

With every pulse, the night transforms,
In waves of glow, the spirit warms,
The northern lights, in silence shout,
Of mysteries that roam about.

Each hue a story, bold, profound,
In nature's grasp, our hearts are bound,
For in the shimmer, we are free,
To share our truths, just you and me.

So look above, as shadows play,
And let the lights show you the way,
For in their glow, we find our spark,
Secrets carried in the dark.

# Echoing Harmonies of the Verdant Realm

In forests deep, where whispers weave,
The songs of nature gently breathe,
Each leaf a note, each brook a chord,
In harmony, our hearts restored.

The trees embrace with arms so wide,
Beneath their shade, our dreams reside,
A symphony of earth and sky,
Together as the years drift by.

With every rustle, tales unfold,
Of hidden worlds, both brave and bold,
The chorus of the greenest glade,
In silent rhythms, joy is made.

The petals dance, a vivid light,
Echoing love in morning's sight,
A tapestry of life anew,
In verdant realms, we find what's true.

So wander forth, where nature calls,
And listen close as beauty sprawls,
For in each sound, a spark ignites,
Echoing harmonies through nights.

## The Lullaby of Enchanted Whispers

In twilight's glow, a hush descends,
A lullaby that softly bends,
Through silky threads of starlit dreams,
Where magic flows in silver streams.

The shadows weave their gentle song,
In rhythmic beats, we all belong,
With every sigh that fills the night,
Enchanted whispers take their flight.

Among the trees, where secrets bloom,
A sweet refrain dispels the gloom,
With every note, the heart awakes,
In melodies that joy remakes.

The moonlight dances on the leaves,
As nature stirs, the spirit breathes,
In gentle tones, we find our peace,
A lullaby that brings release.

So close your eyes and let it soar,
The whispers weave forevermore,
In dreams so deep, your worries fade,
For love's sweet song will never jade.

# Veils of Color in the Wizard's Garden

In gardens vast, where wonders grow,
Veils of color form a show,
With blossoms bright and scents divine,
In magic's grip, all things align.

The petals shimmer, tales unfold,
Of wizards wise and legends bold,
Through every hue, a spell is cast,
In whispers soft, the die is cast.

Beneath the arch of twinkling stars,
The garden breathes, its magic ours,
Each vibrant shade a story spun,
In harmony, we are as one.

From every seed, a dream takes flight,
In twilight's glow and morning's light,
With every step, we find our place,
In wizard's garden, full of grace.

So come and wander, lose your fears,
Amongst the blooms, the laughter cheers,
For in this realm, we're never far,
Veils of color, our guiding star.

## The Enigma Found in Whispering Winds

Beneath the trees, a secret stirs,
The whispers ride on gentle purrs.
A dance of leaves, a cryptic tune,
Where shadows play beneath the moon.

In echoes soft, a tale unfolds,
Of ancient woods and daring bolds.
The breeze, it carries myths untold,
Of wanderers and their dreams of gold.

Each rustling branch, a voice so clear,
Inviting hearts to draw near.
With every gust, the world transforms,
In winds that swirl, the spirit warms.

What secrets lie in nature's breath?
A maze of life, a dance with death.
Within each gust, a heartfelt plea,
To listen close, to let it be.

So wander forth, embrace the strange,
In whispered winds, life finds its range.
The enigma calls, do not resist,
For in its arms, dreams coexist.

## The Lattice of Stars in Enchanted Dreams

At twilight's gate, the cosmos glows,
A tapestry where magic flows.
Each twinkling light, a wish unspun,
In dreams, we chase the setting sun.

Upon the hills, the starlight gleams,
We weave our hopes within our dreams.
The night sky whispers tales of old,
Of love entwined and hearts of gold.

A lattice forms in velvet night,
As ancient songs take majestic flight.
Each constellation tells a tale,
Of journeys vast, where spirits sail.

In shadows cast by moonlit beams,
Awakened hearts feel boundless themes.
The dance of stars, a sight so rare,
Reminds us all, we're free as air.

So let us dream beneath this dome,
In every star, we find a home.
With open souls, we rise, we see,
The lattice sings our destiny.

# The Fluidity of Spirit in Nature's Song

In every brook, the waters swirl,
A symphony unfurls, a pearl.
Each ripple sings, a secret flow,
In liquid notes that softly glow.

The wind it hums through ancient trees,
A melody that stirs the breeze.
The notes of earth, in harmony,
Craft tales of life, wild and free.

In rustling grass, the whispers dance,
Inviting all to join the trance.
With nature's song, our spirits rise,
To seek the truth beneath the skies.

Each petal's fall, a story told,
Of seasons past, of dreams yet bold.
The fluidity of life unfolds,
In every breath, the art of old.

So as you wander, heed the sound,
In nature's voice, our peace is found.
From mountain high to ocean's throng,
Embrace the world in nature's song.

# Confluences of the Arcane Path

In twilight's silence, shadows weave,
Threads of power, unseen, conceive.
Winding paths, both dense and rare,
Whispers of magic fill the air.

With every step, the cosmos bends,
Mysteries beckon, the arcane sends.
Through ancient woods, a journey unspooled,
By moonlit signs, the brave are schooled.

Bewitched by dreams, the heart takes flight,
Drawing near to the dotted light.
The secret lore, in silence, calls,
As guided spirits dance through halls.

Cloaked in wonder, tales enfold,
Adventures rich, and legends bold.
In the dawning of the night's embrace,
We find our truth in this sacred space.

## The Delicate Tangle of Treasures

A tapestry spun of shimmering nights,
Each thread alive with hidden delights.
Curios glimmer, in corners, they shine,
Gathered from worlds, both yours and mine.

In nooks and crannies, secrets lie,
Potions and trinkets that never die.
A feathered charm, a jewel's soft glow,
Stories untold, in each treasure, flow.

Gentle hands craft from shadows and light,
Bestowing purpose on all in sight.
The delicate dance of fate's own hands,
Unearths the wonders in mystical lands.

Wrapped in whispers, the treasures call,
To hearts that listen and spirits enthrall.
Each finding a chapter where dreams intertwine,
In a labyrinth's heart, where paths align.

## Cascades of the Whimsical Spirit

A river of laughter, in colors it sprawls,
Frolicsome echoes within glistening halls.
Jubilant ripples, like sparkles of dew,
Unravel tales, both strange and true.

Dancing in meadows, our worries take flight,
With breezes of joy that twinkle at night.
Through moonlit paths, our shadows embark,
Finding the wonders that flourish in dark.

The whimsy of youth, forever entwined,
In pockets of starlight, where fates are aligned.
Chasing the dreams on a shimmering wave,
Our spirits awakened, neither quiet nor grave.

With each playful twist, life's canvas we paint,
Woven with magic, both wild and quaint.
A cascade of moments, in laughter we share,
The essence of freedom, woven with care.

## Beneath the Veil of Glimmering Motion

A tapestry spun with celestial glow,
We weave through time, where the cosmos flows.
Beneath the stars, in a dance so divine,
The heart learns to listen, the soul learns to shine.

In the realms of the night, secrets take flight,
Magical whispers stir ethereal light.
Veils of mystery flit 'neath the skies,
As dreams reach for heights, where the stardust lies.

Cascading visions of shimmering grace,
In rhythm with time, we embrace the space.
A gentle reminder of all we've known,
In moments of stillness, the truth we have sown.

Beneath glimmers bright, our shadows entwine,
In the softest embrace, where destinies align.
Through the ebb and flow, the spirals of fate,
Reveal the beauty that lies in the state.

# Enchantment's Breath on a Wistful Evening

A whisper floats on twilight's sigh,
As shadows dance 'neath the starry sky.
The world holds breath in a hush so sweet,
While magic stirs on the cobbled street.

Old trees murmur secrets of old,
Their bark adorned with stories bold.
The lanterns flicker with gentle glow,
Where dreams may linger and moments flow.

In corners where the faeries play,
The moonlight weaves through night and day.
With every glimmer, hopes ignite,
A tapestry of sheer delight.

The echo of laughter, soft and clear,
Weaves through the air like music near.
With every sigh, a heart shall know,
Enchantment's breath in the evening's show.

## The Vision of a Shimmering Fable

Upon the edge of dreams unfurled,
A vision stirs in a hidden world.
Where stories dance in radiant light,
And fables take their wondrous flight.

Through verdant glades, the visions roam,
In whispers sweet, they find a home.
With silver threads the tales are spun,
Beneath the gaze of a gentle sun.

A tapestry of colors bright,
Awakens hearts to pure delight.
With starlit wishes and murmured lore,
The magic beckons, forevermore.

Eyes glisten with every turn,
As tales unfold and passions burn.
The shimmering fable, a guiding star,
Leading us onward, no matter how far.

## The Pulse of Serenity on the Breeze

In the quiet corners where silence dwells,
The pulse of serenity softly swells.
Like gentle waves upon the shore,
It wraps the weary in sweetness galore.

Whispers of nature sway in the air,
Each breath a blessing, tender and rare.
The world around, in harmony blends,
Where every moment, the spirit mends.

With rustling leaves, the breezes play,
A soothing song at the end of day.
In the warmth of dusk, the heart takes flight,
Carried by dreams into the night.

Where worries fade with the setting sun,
And peace is found, the journey begun.
The pulse of serenity, a gentle guide,
In nature's embrace, we abide.

# Glimpse of the Unexpected in the Fey Realm

In shadows deep where secrets lie,
A glimpse of magic flits on by.
With laughter ringing through the glade,
The fey realm glimmers, unafraid.

Where flowers bloom in colors rare,
And time drifts lightly on fragrant air.
The whispers of beings, bold and slight,
Dance in the corners, hidden from sight.

A shimmer catches the wandering eye,
As dreams and wishes seem to fly.
With every flutter, hearts align,
In this realm where wonders intertwine.

Each step a marvel, each breath a thrill,
As magic thrums through the softest chill.
In twilight's embrace, the unexpected gleams,
Rich with the essence of whispered dreams.

# Enchanted Paths of the Velvet Moon

Beneath the glow of silver beams,
Whispers dance through shadowed dreams,
Where secrets veil the ancient trees,
And night unveils her mysteries.

Each step upon the mossy ground,
Echoes softly, a haunting sound,
The velvet moon, a watchful eye,
Guides wanderers as they stroll by.

In shimmering pools of midnight's grace,
Reflections shimmer, time's embrace,
With every breath, the magic grows,
As starlit wind through branches blows.

Crickets weave their quiet tune,
A symphony beneath the moon,
In this enchanted, twilight sphere,
Hearts awaken, free from fear.

So wander close, let spirits soar,
Embrace the night forevermore,
For on these paths, where dreams align,
The velvet moon shall always shine.

## Ripples of Laughter Beneath the Leaves

In shaded glades where shadows play,
Children's laughter fills the day,
Beneath the boughs, beneath the skies,
Joyful echoes softly rise.

Leaves that dance to breezes light,
Carry giggles, pure delight,
The world transformed in vibrant hues,
As nature hums its joyful muse.

With every rustle, secrets shared,
A tapestry of dreams prepared,
Adventures born in forest's heart,
Where every soul can take a part.

Here, whispers float like morning mist,
In every moment, none are missed,
Connected by the laughter's art,
A harmony that won't depart.

So linger here, amid the trees,
And feel the magic in the breeze,
For in this place where laughter weaves,
Life's sweetest melody believes.

## Symphony of Enigma in Nature's Heart

The dawn awakens, soft and bright,
Nature hums with pure delight,
Each creature sings its own refrain,
In whispered notes, a sweet campaign.

Shadows mingle with the light,
Secrets held both day and night,
Mysteries in the rustling leaves,
In every heart, a magic weaves.

The brook murmurs its ancient song,
As time winds through its endless throng,
In mirrored depths, reflections gleam,
Unraveling the fabric of a dream.

Songs of petals in the breeze,
Rustle gently through the trees,
Every scent and sound a clue,
In nature's heart, a world anew.

So listen close, and you shall find,
The language shared by all mankind,
In the symphony of nature's art,
The echo dwells within your heart.

## The Gentle Push of Enchanted Breezes

A whisper glides on emerald air,
Brushing softly, without a care,
The gentle push of breath so light,
Invoking dreams that take to flight.

Through fields of gold and skies of blue,
Wandering hearts with visions new,
Each breeze a secret, sweetly spun,
Under the gaze of the radiant sun.

The petals dance as winds embrace,
A playful waltz in time and space,
In every gust, a tale unfolds,
A love for life that never molds.

Beneath the clouds, a fleeting trace,
Of laughter found in nature's grace,
So let the breezes lead the way,
To where our spirits long to play.

For in that fleeting, fleeting breeze,
Lie endless hopes, like autumn leaves,
Embrace the thrill of journeys vast,
With playful winds, we're free at last.

# Symphony of Enigma in Nature's Heart

The dawn awakens, soft and bright,
Nature hums with pure delight,
Each creature sings its own refrain,
In whispered notes, a sweet campaign.

Shadows mingle with the light,
Secrets held both day and night,
Mysteries in the rustling leaves,
In every heart, a magic weaves.

The brook murmurs its ancient song,
As time winds through its endless throng,
In mirrored depths, reflections gleam,
Unraveling the fabric of a dream.

Songs of petals in the breeze,
Rustle gently through the trees,
Every scent and sound a clue,
In nature's heart, a world anew.

So listen close, and you shall find,
The language shared by all mankind,
In the symphony of nature's art,
The echo dwells within your heart.

# The Gentle Push of Enchanted Breezes

A whisper glides on emerald air,
Brushing softly, without a care,
The gentle push of breath so light,
Invoking dreams that take to flight.

Through fields of gold and skies of blue,
Wandering hearts with visions new,
Each breeze a secret, sweetly spun,
Under the gaze of the radiant sun.

The petals dance as winds embrace,
A playful waltz in time and space,
In every gust, a tale unfolds,
A love for life that never molds.

Beneath the clouds, a fleeting trace,
Of laughter found in nature's grace,
So let the breezes lead the way,
To where our spirits long to play.

For in that fleeting, fleeting breeze,
Lie endless hopes, like autumn leaves,
Embrace the thrill of journeys vast,
With playful winds, we're free at last.

## Magic Sparkling in the Evening Air

In twilight's breath, the world transforms,
With whispers soft and gentle swarms.
The stars awake, their lanterns bright,
Illuminating dreams that take flight.

A shimmer dances on the breeze,
Carrying secrets through the trees.
Moonbeams weave through branches bare,
Where magic sparkles in the air.

The shadows stretch and softly sigh,
As fireflies twinkle, floating by.
Each flicker holds a story true,
Of wonders waiting just for you.

With heart alight and spirits free,
Embrace the night, a mystery.
For in this realm of soft delight,
The magic glows, a pure insight.

So let the evening charm your soul,
As moonlight bathes you whole and whole.
With every breath, let hope declare,
A dance of dreams in evening air.

## The Flute of the Silvered Woods

Amidst the trees, where shadows play,
A haunting tune begins to sway.
The flute of silver, soft and clear,
Calls forth the magic, draws it near.

The leaves respond with rustling sounds,
As if enchanted by the grounds.
With every note, the forest wakes,
And ancient secrets it remakes.

A spirit lost, now found in song,
Guides weary hearts that drift along.
Each melody invokes a past,
A timeless dance, so fair and vast.

With every breath, the music flows,
Through mossy paths where no one goes.
The flute still sings, a gentle call,
In silvered woods where dreams enthrall.

So pause and listen, let it be,
The magic lives in harmony.
For in the woods, the flute shall play,
A tune of wonder, night or day.

# Tides of Enchantment in the Evening Glow

When sun dips low and waters gleam,
The tides awaken from their dream.
A shimmer spreads across the shore,
Where waves embrace the sea once more.

Each crest and fall, a spell is cast,
Whispers of joy, a spell recast.
In every tide, a story flows,
Of worlds unseen, where magic glows.

As seagulls dance on breezy flights,
The evening sky ignites with lights.
A canvas painted, rich and bright,
With hues of wonder, pure delight.

As twilight settles, shadows play,
The ocean hums a lullaby sway.
Each wave a heartbeat, each splash a sigh,
In tides of love, our spirits fly.

So linger long, let moments stay,
In evening's glow, let worries fray.
For in the sea and sky's embrace,
Enchantment lives, a timeless space.

# The Awakened Spirit in the Silken Shadows

In silken shadows, soft and deep,
A spirit stirs from ancient sleep.
With whispered grace, it walks the night,
Unraveling dreams, a wondrous sight.

Through moonlit paths, it glides with ease,
Caressing leaves, and dancing trees.
A heartbeat echoes, softly clear,
Awakening hopes we hold so dear.

In every corner, whispers play,
A gentle touch, a guiding ray.
For those who seek, the spirit calls,
In silken shadows, no one falls.

Gather your courage, let it soar,
And find the magic at your door.
With every step, the night unfurls,
A dance of dreams in stardust swirls.

So trust the path that winds so true,
The spirit shines, awaiting you.
In every shadow, light shall grow,
Awakened dreams in vibrant flow.

# Ethereal Threads of a Forgotten Melody

Softly woven in twilight's breath,
Whispers of dreams begin to weave,
A melody lost in the arms of death,
Each note a sigh that won't leave.

In shadows where secrets softly lie,
The echoes dance in a gentle swirl,
They call to the heart with a tender cry,
Unfurling the magic of the world.

Through gossamer threads that shimmer bright,
The fabric of time starts to bend,
As starlit wishes take sudden flight,
Each moment a spark that will not end.

Legacies found in the silken air,
Threads weave stories of ages past,
To unravel the weight of burdens rare,
In whispers of melody, unsurpassed.

Rekindling the fire of long-lost bliss,
With every sigh, a chance to reclaim,
The rhythm that still haunts our tender kiss,
Ethereal threads, igniting the flame.

# Whimsical Turns of the Mystic Brook

Where willows cry and waters flow,
In moonlit glimmers by the stone,
The brook sings low, where soft winds blow,
A secret world, the brook's own throne.

Through twists and turns, where shadows flit,
The laughter of fairies fills the night,
Each ripple stirs in a dance, a wit,
A whimsical chase, a pure delight.

Wildflowers bloom beneath the arch,
A tapestry woven of colors bright,
Where time is lost and dreams embark,
In the gentle embrace of silver light.

Each drop a tale, a soft embrace,
The brook, a storyteller at play,
It knows the way, it knows our grace,
Guiding our hearts to a brighter day.

In emerald depths, where secrets dwell,
The whispering waters will always gleam,
In each twist, a story to tell,
The brook will carry us where we dream.

# Illumination of Medieval Dreams

In castles tall with ivy dressed,
The echoes of knights retrieve the past,
In candlelight, their stories rest,
A vibrant tapestry unsurpassed.

The banners flutter, colors bright,
Each whisper hangs in the air so sweet,
As shadows dance through the velvet night,
Ancient vows on a heart's heartbeat.

In hidden chambers, secrets lie,
Where lovers meet with a stolen glance,
Their hopes entwined as the stars reply,
Illuminating a timeless dance.

Through echoes of laughter, dreams resound,
In every stone, a tale enfolds,
Of gallant hearts and love profound,
The magic of history gently molds.

In parchment scrolls and quills of gold,
The dreams awaken with each new dawn,
A tapestry woven with tales retold,
In medieval hues, forever drawn.

# Comets Sliding Through a Painted Sky

Brushstrokes of color, vibrant and bold,
Comets trace pathways on canvas high,
Their stories of wonder in stardust told,
As dreams take flight through the painted sky.

Dancing on whispers of cosmic lace,
They glide through mysteries, ancient and vast,
A luminous trail, a celestial race,
Comets of promise, steadfast and fast.

Beneath the gaze of a watchful night,
Hearts twinkle bright in the cosmos' glow,
Each flicker a wish on a canvas of light,
As dreams are born in the dark ebb and flow.

With every arc, new stories are spun,
As time slips softly into the unknown,
Their brilliance a mark of the day just begun,
A reminder that we are never alone.

So, let us wander where starlight streams,
In the vast expanse of the sweeping wide,
To chase our fate and to cradle our dreams,
Comets sliding through the painted sky.

# Floating Notes of a Hidden Realm

In whispers soft as morning dew,
A melody rides the sighing breeze,
From valleys deep to skies so blue,
Each note a tale, each chord a tease.

Spirits weave through the emerald trees,
With laughter bright as fireflies' glow,
Their voices blend, a sweet reprise,
In secret corners, worlds we know.

The brook hums low with ancient lore,
While shadows dance beneath the moon,
Entwined in dreams we can't ignore,
Their magic thrums—a tender tune.

Cloaked in night, the forest sways,
As echoes call from long ago,
Each quiet footstep we relays,
A symphony of hearts aglow.

So linger here, let time suspend,
In whispering woods, our worries cease,
For every note, a faithful friend,
In floating notes, we find our peace.

## The Dance of Flavors in the Air

A dash of spice in morning light,
The fragrant herbs, they twirl and sway,
With citrus bright, a sheer delight,
In kitchens warm, the senses play.

The sizzle sings in frying pans,
As laughter linger, aromas rise,
Each taste a tale from distant lands,
In unity, the palate flies.

Sweet drizzles of honey weave through,
With savory hints of garlic's grace,
A dance of flavors, old and new,
Each bite a smile, each sip a embrace.

Textures melt like dreams unfurled,
On tongues that savor every hue,
In feasts, we travel, hearts entwined,
With stories shared from me to you.

So gather 'round, let joy proclaim,
In every dish, a tale to share,
United by this tasty game,
In the dance of flavors, our souls declare.

## Glimmers Beneath the Starlit Canopy

Beneath the stars, where dreams take flight,
A silver glimmer in the night air,
The cosmos whispers, soft and bright,
With secrets held in every stare.

The moon spills light on whispered sighs,
As night winds weave through leafy boughs,
Each star a wish, a lullaby,
In twilight's clutch, the heart allows.

Soft shadows play on dewy grass,
Where fireflies blink in syncopate,
And time, it bends—a fleeting pass,
In every twinkle, a universe waits.

The night is rich with stories told,
In every twinkling, tales unfold,
We find ourselves, both brave and bold,
In glimmers soft, our hearts consoled.

So let us dance beneath the skies,
And weave our hopes with each bright star,
For in this space, our spirits rise,
In starlit dreams, we're never far.

## Mysteries Weaved in Gossamer Threads

In twilight's glow, a tapestry,
Of whispers hushed and secrets spun,
With gossamer, life's mystery,
Each thread a tale, a life begun.

The spider dances, deftly bright,
Her artistry, a fragile song,
In silken strands, a magic light,
Where shadows play, and dreams belong.

Secrets wrapped in twilight's shawl,
As moonlit paths begin to blur,
In each soft whisper, we enthrall,
The wanderers, the seekers stir.

Unraveled knots of fate intertwine,
With every breath, the stories plead,
A glimpse of wonder, ether divine,
In the tapestry, our hearts all heed.

So linger long in this quiet space,
Where mysteries dance, and stories thrive,
In gossamer threads, find solace, grace,
For in these webs, our dreams survive.

# Mirage of the Arcane Tides

In twilight's glow the waters gleam,
Whispers dance upon the stream,
Shadows weave a mystic thread,
As dreams of old begin to spread.

The tides roll back, revealing light,
Secrets lost to darkest night,
In every wave a story waits,
A spellbound heart, the ocean's fate.

Amidst the mist a vision glows,
Of heroes past the current flows,
With every crest, an echo calls,
To seek the magic that enthralls.

A siren's song, both sweet and dire,
Awakens depths, ignites the fire,
To sail beyond the world we know,
And seek the realm where wonders grow.

So heed the call of waters wide,
Let not your courage slip and hide,
For in the waves of destiny,
The mirage bends to sets you free.

## Surrender to the Twisting Vortex

A storm approaches, dark and vast,
The swirling might of shadows cast,
A spiral deep where secrets weave,
And in its heart, you must believe.

On edges sharp and pathways dim,
The whispers beckon, soft and grim,
Embrace the pull, let senses flare,
For in the chaos, find your care.

The swirling winds, a dance of fate,
A portal opened, no escape,
Yet strength resides in tides unknown,
A journey carved, a fate outgrown.

When time unfolds the fractured line,
Embrace the clash, the grand design,
For through the storm, the truth will shine,
In shadows deep, your stars align.

With every twist, the heart will soar,
To realms unseen, to distant shore,
Surrender now, let currents guide,
Within the storm, your dreams abide.

## The Song of the Spiraling Mist

In morning's breath, the mist will sing,
A melody that stirs the springs,
With every note, a tale is spun,
Of light and darkness—two as one.

The gossamer drapes the forest floor,
As wisps of magic weave and soar,
In every swirl a story twines,
Of forgotten realms where hope aligns.

So close your eyes, and breathe it in,
Feel every whisper from within,
Let fragments dance in air so sweet,
As nature's chorus finds its beat.

Though shadows hide in folds of gray,
The mist unveils what dreams convey,
With laughter ringing through the trees,
The spiraling song will bring you peace.

In every wave of silvered haze,
A symphony of love ablaze,
Hear now the call of the untouched,
And walk the path the mist has brushed.

## Luminous Trails of Elven Laughter

Beneath the boughs where shadows play,
The laughter of the elves holds sway,
A twinkling light in twilight's grasp,
As joy unfolds in a playful clasp.

With every step on soft mossed ground,
A melody of magic found,
Their voices blend with night's embrace,
Creating warmth in this sacred space.

In laughter shared, the world ignites,
A flicker bright that lights the nights,
As stars above begin to dance,
In every heart, a wistful chance.

The trails they leave in silver streams,
Are echoes caught in whimsical dreams,
As nature hums in sweet reply,
Each joyful note, a gentle sigh.

So wander here, where spirits glow,
And bask within the love they show,
For in this realm of laughter round,
The light of life is always found.

# By the Firelight of Enchanted Realms

In the hearth's embrace, tales unfold,
Of wizards brave and spirits bold.
Crackling whispers weave through the night,
Guiding lost souls to realms of light.

Flickering flames in a dance so bright,
Illuminate dreams that take to flight.
Shadows twist in a wondrous play,
Guardians of secrets in the glowing sway.

Around the fire, laughter and song,
Echoes of journeys where we belong.
A tapestry of hearts, woven tight,
By the firelight, all feels right.

Mysterious paths beckon us near,
In the warmth of magic, we shed our fear.
With every flicker, a story unveiled,
In enchanted realms, our spirits hailed.

So gather close, let the embers guide,
Through the night, with magic as our ride.
For every heartbeat, a promise made,
By the firelight, adventures cascaded.

## Gentle Undulations of Moonlit Seas

Under the moon's soft, silver beam,
The ocean whispers a haunting dream.
Waves like lullabies kiss the shore,
In their embrace, we crave for more.

Nights of magic with sails unfurled,
A dance of tides in a slumbering world.
Stars twinkle above, a celestial guide,
On gentle undulations, we choose to ride.

The sea's sweet sighs in the cool night air,
Secrets of mermaids linger everywhere.
Whispers of joy, both tender and true,
In moonlit caresses, a love anew.

As the horizon blends shades of blue,
Every ripple carries a story, too.
In the depths of dreams, we find our way,
With the ocean's heart, we wish to stay.

So sail away on this tranquil sea,
Where moonlight dances and sets us free.
For in these waves, our spirits rise,
In gentle undulations, beneath the skies.

# The Arcane Dance of Light and Shadow

In the twilight hour, secrets awake,
The dance of shadows, a spell to make.
Flickers of light ignite the scene,
In the balance of dark, the magic unseen.

Whispers of wind tell tales long lost,
Of ancient powers and the line crossed.
With every heartbeat, the shadows breathe,
In the arcane dance, their truths we weave.

Draped in twilight, where silence reigns,
The tapestry of life reveals its veins.
Light and shadow, a harmonious blend,
In this mystic waltz, we find our end.

Step lightly now, through realms unknown,
As stars align and our fears are sown.
In the sway of night, we lose control,
The arcane dance awakens the soul.

So take my hand, let the magic flow,
Through every flicker, embrace the glow.
For in the shadows, we find our glow,
In the arcane dance, together we go.

## Patterns of Wonder in a Twilight's Glow

In twilight's glow, the world transforms,
Shapes and patterns in gentle swarms.
The sky blushes in hues so rare,
We stand in awe of the beauty there.

Silhouettes flicker, like dreams untold,
In the breathless moments, we silently behold.
Nature's canvas, painted with grace,
Each stroke a memory, each glance a trace.

As fireflies twinkle, the night awakes,
Each flicker of light, a journey it makes.
The whispers of leaves, a soft serenade,
In patterns of wonder, our fears cascade.

From mountains high to valleys deep,
The secrets of twilight our hearts will keep.
With every sigh of the cooling breeze,
We find our solace among the trees.

So let us wander, hand in hand,
Through magical realms, both vast and grand.
For in twilight's embrace, we'll forever stay,
In patterns of wonder, come what may.

## Whispers of Enchanted Curves

In twilight's glow the fae do play,
With laughter soft as shadows sway.
Their grace bestowed on fields so wide,
Where mystery and magic bide.

The breeze carries tales from afar,
Of hidden realms where wonders are.
Through sighing leaves and silver streams,
Dancing between reality and dreams.

Upon the path, the moonlight weaves,
The secrets whispered by the leaves.
A shimmer lingers in the air,
A touch of magic everywhere.

In every twist and every turn,
Are stories waiting, hearts that yearn.
The curves enchant, they softly call,
To wanderers who dare to fall.

Embrace the glow, the night's embrace,
Find solace in this sacred space.
For in the quiet, truths unfurl,
In whispers of enchanted curves.

## The Melody of Mystic Clouds

Up high where dreams and stardust meet,
The clouds compose a symphony sweet.
With each soft note of silver rain,
They sing of hope and joy unrestrained.

A curtain drawn on the azure stage,
They dance upon an endless page.
In gentle swirls of cotton white,
They cradle secrets of the night.

The whispers of the winds descend,
With tales of ages that won't end.
Through vibrant hues of dawn's embrace,
Each cloud a story, each shape a grace.

So close your eyes and hear the song,
Of timeless skies where you belong.
Embrace the dreams that float above,
In the melody of mystic love.

Let each soft puffy form enthrall,
As breezes weave their magic call.
With every breath, the world unbound,
Echoes the beauty that's all around.

## Dance of the Ethereal Elk

In twilight's hush, the forest breathes,
As shadows play beneath the leaves.
With antlers crowned in silver glow,
The elk prances where wildflowers grow.

Each step a whisper, soft and sweet,
A rhythm set by nature's beat.
They leap through mist, a ballet rare,
In sacred woods, they find their lair.

Beneath the stars, their spirits soar,
A circle formed, forever more.
In moonlit glades, they twist and twirl,
Awakening the night to whirl.

The echoes of the nightingale,
Guide their steps through the gleaming veil.
An ethereal beauty, strong and bold,
A story of wildness yet untold.

As dawn awakes with rosy hue,
The dance concludes, but still feels new.
In hearts of those who witnessed well,
Lives on the magic of the elk's spell.

## Secrets in the Currents of Stardust


Across the night, a river flows,
Of stardust secrets no one knows.
In whispers carried by the breeze,
Lies a magic under trees.

The night unveils its sparkling tales,
In shades where starlight softly pales.
With every flicker, stories gleam,
A tapestry woven from dreams.

In currents deep, mysteries stir,
Telling tales that we defer.
Each spark a wish, each wish a chance,
To join the cosmos in a dance.

So heed the calls from realms above,
With an open heart, embrace the love.
For in the universe, truth persists,
In secrets found in stardust mists.

As day breaks forth, glimmers retreat,
Yet in our souls, the magic's beat.
The currents flow, forever free,
Whispering secrets, just for me.

# A Twist of Fate in the Fairy's Dance


In twilight's grasp, the fairies play,
With shimmering wings, they weave their way.
A spark of laughter, a fleeting glance,
The magic stirs in their mystic dance.

Beneath the boughs, where shadows creep,
Secrets whispered, the heart will leap.
With every twirl, a chance is spun,
In the glow of stars, the night's begun.

A twist of fate, the night unfolds,
In shimmering silk, stories are told.
With each soft flutter, a wish takes flight,
In the fairy's dance, magic is bright.

The moonlight shimmers, casting spells,
In the soft breeze, the silence dwells.
Through veils of night, they dance and sway,
Eternal dreams in a fleeting play.

In twilight's grasp, new paths are found,
Where laughter echoes, joy abounds.
A twist of fate, the fairies prance,
In a world where dreams forever dance.

# The Chime of Dreams Upon Water's Edge

By the water's edge, the lilies bloom,
With whispers soft, dispelling gloom.
The chime of dreams calls out at dusk,
In fragrant air, the world is husk.

A silver stream reflects the sky,
Where wishes linger, never shy.
Each ripple dances, tales untold,
In harmony with dreams of gold.

Beneath the gaze of stars aglow,
The rivers hum, their secrets flow.
A gentle breeze, a soft embrace,
Where time meanders, finding grace.

With whispers sweet, the night draws near,
In darkness veiled, the heart feels clear.
Each flicker soft, each shadow blends,
In the chime of dreams, where magic bends.

Upon the shore, the twilight gleams,
A gateway forged from silent dreams.
The water's edge, where hopes arise,
In that soft glow, the spirit flies.

## Murmurs of Magic Within the Forest

In ancient woods, the whispers tell,
Of secrets deep, where spirits dwell.
Each rustling leaf, a tale unfolds,
In murmurs soft, the forest holds.

The twilight shadows, painted hues,
In amber lights, enchantment brews.
With every step, the magic stirs,
As winding paths twist like soft purrs.

Beneath the boughs, where silence breathes,
The stories caught in webbed leaves.
Each footfall soft, the echoes weave,
In nature's heart, we dare believe.

From every root and every stone,
The pulse of life is gently sown.
In hallowed groves, the heart will seek,
The spark of magic, quiet, meek.

In hidden smiles and glistening dew,
The whispers dance, the magic brew.
A world unseen, where wonders thrive,
In murmurs of magic, the forest's alive.

# The Serpent's Dance in the Moonlit Glow

Beneath the stars, a serpent glides,
In silken moves, where darkness hides.
The moonlit glow casts shadows wide,
In nature's song, the dreams abide.

With emerald scales and eyes like fire,
The serpent sways, a whispered choir.
Each twist and turn, a spell is cast,
In rhythm deep, the night holds fast.

Through tangled brush and thorny way,
Where secrets stir and spirits play.
With every breath, the night transforms,
In silence deep, a magic warms.

In moonlit shimmer, time slows near,
A dance of shadows, crystal clear.
With every glide, the magic spins,
In the serpent's dance, the night begins.

Where echoes linger, and dreams entwine,
The pulse of night, the stars align.
In the dance of serpents, bold and bright,
The whispers of magic kiss the night.

## Colorful Shifts of a Magical Vine

In twilight's glow, the colors blend,
A vine awakens, dreams descend.
Its tendrils weave through the dampened air,
Whispers of magic linger there.

Beneath the arching leaves divine,
A tapestry flows, rich and fine.
Hues of emerald, ruby, and gold,
Stories of wonder in silence told.

Each twist revealing hidden lore,
Of faeries' dances on the floor.
With every bloom, a secret sigh,
Awaits the night, the stars nearby.

The vine, alive with tales to speak,
In shadows deep, the curious seek.
A realm where fantasies entwine,
Behold the beauty, soft, benign.

As day departs, the whispers grow,
Embracing hearts in ebb and flow.
In vibrant shades, let spirits pry,
These colorful shifts don't say goodbye.

# Beneath the Canopy of Distant Stars

A canopy of night unfolds,
In twinkling lights, the magic holds.
Beneath the sky of velvet blue,
Dreams take flight, both old and new.

The breeze carries a hush so deep,
As woodland secrets softly seep.
Through rustling leaves, sweet echoes call,
Inviting all who dare to fall.

A journey starts with hearts aligned,
As stars above play tricks on mind.
Each glowing orb, a wish bestowed,
Under this vast, enchanted road.

The shadows dance, the owls in flight,
Guarding whispers of the night.
In every glimmer, silence sings,
Of fairytales and ancient things.

As dawn approaches, colors blend,
The stars retreat, their night-time friend.
Yet in our hearts, they stay ajar,
Forever bright, those distant stars.

## Fantasies Unfurled in Dream's Embrace

In realms where dreams align with fate,
Fantasies flourish, never late.
With gentle brush of evening's wing,
Magic bursts forth, as wishes sing.

A tapestry of sights and sounds,
Where hopes take root in grassy grounds.
The air thick with an ether's glow,
Of whispered secrets, soft and slow.

Each corner holds a mirrored past,
Reflections of a spell once cast.
With every turn, new wonders peek,
In vibrant colors, joy does speak.

Embrace the journey, twist and twine,
In depths forgotten, truth may shine.
For in this space where dreams entwine,
The heart remembers, love's design.

As morning rays prepare to greet,
The dreams held close, no swift retreat.
In every heartbeat, magic's trace,
Nestled deep in dream's embrace.

# Echoing Laughter of the Woodland Spirits

In wooded glens, a laughter rings,
With echoes light as autumn's wings.
The spirits dance with mirthful grace,
In dappled sunlight, find their place.

Through tangled roots and fragrant blooms,
Their joy lifts hearts, dispels all glooms.
With every step on golden leaves,
The forest shares what magic weaves.

As twilight falls, the shadows play,
In vibrant shades, they weave the day.
Each rustle holds a story spun,
Of ancient tales, of moonlit fun.

The woodland sways to nature's song,
In unity, they all belong.
With every whisper, laughter swells,
In harmony, the woodland dwells.

As stars awaken one by one,
The joyous dance never is done.
In echoes, laughter lingers near,
Embracing hearts, dispelling fear.

# The Journey of a Wisp Through the Canopy

In twilight's glow, a wisp takes flight,
Through tangled branches, soft and light.
It dances high on whispered breeze,
Among the leaves, it sways with ease.

The forest hums, a lullaby,
Where shadows play and secrets lie.
As moonbeams filter through the air,
The wisp explores with tender care.

It glimmers bright in dappled shade,
A spirit bold, a friend unmade.
Through ancient woods, it weaves and twirls,
A guardian of enchanted worlds.

With every pulse, the night unfolds,
A tale of joy, a heart that holds.
Guided by stars, the journey new,
A wisp of dreams, forever true.

As dawn awakes, the shadows fade,
With mist and light, the path is laid.
Yet in the heart, the forest stays,
A journey marked by magic ways.

## Enchanted Waves that Kiss the Shoreline

Beneath the sun, the ocean gleams,
A tapestry of woven dreams.
The waves that dance with playful grace,
Embrace the shore, a sweet embrace.

They whisper tales of distant lands,
Of ships and sails, and gentle hands.
Each rolling swell, a voice so clear,
Invites the heart to linger near.

The seagulls cry, a raucous cheer,
As golden shores draw wanderers near.
With sandy toes and salt-kissed skin,
The magic of the sea draws in.

At sunset's blush, the sky aglow,
The waves reflect a fiery show.
In colors bold, the day does die,
While moonlit whispers fill the sky.

The tide ebbs low, then surges high,
A rhythm strong, where spirits fly.
In every crest, a secret lies,
As enchanted waves weave lullabies.

# Secrets Hidden Beneath the Sapphire Sky

Beneath the vast and endless hue,
Lie secrets old, yet fresh and new.
With every cloud that drifts above,
A whispered tale of hope and love.

A curtain drawn 'twixt earth and stars,
Where dreams take flight, and free are scars.
In twilight's gaze, a promise shines,
That in the dark, the light still finds.

The winds may carry stories far,
From distant shores to where you are.
With every gust, a truth appears,
A melody that calms all fears.

As day gives way to evening's charm,
And crickets sing with nature's balm,
Look to the sky, and you shall see,
The hidden truths that set hearts free.

For in the fabric of the night,
Lie wonders waiting for the light.
Secrets woven in the stars,
Beneath the sapphire sky, they're ours.

# The Weavings of an Elvish Tale

In ancient woods where shadows play,
The voices weave a tale today.
Of elven kin and moonlit streams,
They dance within our waking dreams.

With silver threads of starlit song,
The stories echo, rich and strong.
Of forests deep and mountains high,
Where magic twirls beneath the sky.

Each leaf that falls, a whisper shared,
Of hearts entwined and souls laid bare.
The paths they tread shout tales of yore,
Of battles fought and love's sweet score.

In twilight's glow, the magic glows,
As time unfurls, the legend grows.
With every breath, the world awakes,
To elvish songs that night remakes.

So gather close, let tales unfold,
In every word, a gem of gold.
For in the weavings of the night,
An elvish tale spins pure delight.

# Enigmatic Movements of the Ethereal Wind

Whispers weave through ancient trees,
Carrying secrets on the breeze.
A dance unseen, yet felt so near,
In every sigh, a tale is clear.

Invisible hands around us glide,
With laughter soft, like moonlit tide.
A flicker here, a shadow there,
The wind's embrace, a curious flair.

In twilight's grasp, the stories spin,
Subtle magic held within.
While starlit skies sing with delight,
The winds enchant the coming night.

Listen close to nature's song,
Where unseen currents all belong.
For in the air, a truth unfolds,
The heart of wind, the world beholds.

# The Tapestry of Enchantment's Flow

Threads of light in twilight's weave,
Entwined with dreams that dare believe.
In patterns bright, the magic swirls,
A dance of fate through time unfurls.

Illusions crafted from the air,
Whispers linger, soft as prayer.
With every twist, a story blooms,
Enigmas lost in shadowed rooms.

The fabric feels like starlit dawn,
Where hopes are stitched and fears are drawn.
Each strand a wish, each hue a thought,
In the tapestry, the soul is sought.

Ethereal threads, so deftly sewn,
Binding hearts in ways unknown.
As dreams entwine in this grand show,
The world is spun from enchantment's flow.

## Choreography of the Mystic Night

Underneath a velvet sky,
Stars perform, they leap and fly.
In shadows deep, the night does dance,
With secrets wrapped in moonlight's glance.

Time stands still in this embrace,
Each moment holds a timeless grace.
With every twirl, the spirits soar,
In the silence, they implore.

The soft glow paints the world anew,
Where every glance holds magic's view.
A choreography of light and sound,
In sacred night, lost thoughts are found.

The night sways on with gentle ease,
Like whispers carried on the breeze.
This mystic show will never cease,
As dreams entwine and hearts find peace.

## Celestial Rhythms in a Dreamscape


Beyond the veil of waking thoughts,
Celestial rhythms weave what's sought.
In shimmering realms of pure delight,
The heart beats softly through the night.

Echoes of stars like distant chimes,
Resonate through timeless rhymes.
A cosmic dance of fate and chance,
In dreamscape's depths, we dare to prance.

Floating on a misty sea,
Where visions roam wild and free.
Each pulse of light, a story told,
In vibrant hues of blue and gold.

Cascading thoughts like rivers flow,
To realms where only dreamers go.
We twirl through galaxies in play,
In this vast night, we lose our way.

## The Spellbound Path of Serendipity

Once upon a moonlit night,
Wanderers tread with hearts so light.
Whispers call from shadows dim,
As fate unfolds on a silken whim.

A twinkle here, a spark anew,
Paths entwine where hope breaks through.
Hidden doors in ivy steep,
Guard secrets the forest keep.

Through crystal streams the pixies dance,
In every glance, a fleeting chance.
Nature's brush paints tales untold,
In vibrant hues of green and gold.

When stars align and wishes soar,
Life's surprises open doors.
In laughter shared, in dreams set free,
The path of joy is meant to be.

So follow where the wild winds blow,
For serendipity's gentle glow.
What lies ahead, none can predict,
In every step, the heart's soft flick.

## Celestial Bends of Myriad Colors

Above the clouds where dreams take flight,
A canvas spreads in soft twilight.
Brushstrokes weave through starry skies,
Where colors melt and magic lies.

Indigo whispers and emerald sings,
Paint the world with vibrant rings.
Sunset hues in dances blend,
As daylight bows to night's sweet end.

Lilac clouds drift, softly sigh,
While golden stars begin to cry.
Each glimmer holds a story bright,
Of worlds unseen and pure delight.

Celestial music swells and sways,
Guiding hearts through starlit bays.
In every hue, a memory wakes,
In every bend, the magic takes.

So look above when shadows creep,
Embrace the colors, dive so deep.
For in the heavens, we shall find,
A tapestry that binds mankind.

## The Enchanted Ripple of Time

In a glade where silence weaves,
Time drifts softly, like autumn leaves.
Each moment glistens, tender, shy,
A whispered tale that floats on by.

Ripples dance on a silver stream,
Echoes shimmer of a forgotten dream.
Fragments alive, a fleeting spark,
Awakens hearts within the dark.

Chronicles of laughter, shadows long,
Composed in nature's sweetest song.
Every heartbeat fills the air,
With magic spun from gentle care.

Yet time does not stand still, you see,
It bends and shifts, wild and free.
Through every glance, a wisp of fate,
In its embrace, we celebrate.

So wander where the moments glide,
In time's embrace, let dreams reside.
For every ripple tells a story,
Of love, of loss, and whispered glory.

# Melodies of the Star-Kissed Forest

Amidst the trees where shadows play,
A symphony of night and day.
Rustling leaves with secrets hum,
In the forest, magic comes.

Moonbeams guide the weary traveler,
Lighting paths to dreams unravel.
Crickets chirp in rhythmic tune,
Beneath the watchful, gentle moon.

Murmurs soft from stars above,
Embrace the heart, a bond of love.
Every branch and every vine,
Echo songs, both old and divine.

As twilight sighs into the dawn,
Nature sings, our worries gone.
With every note, the forest breathes,
A promise held in whispered leaves.

So listen close, let go, unwind,
In melodies, our souls we find.
For in the woods, we're never lost,
Just listening to the songs we've crossed.

## Shimmers of the Twilight Breeze

In twilight's glow, the whispers play,
Beneath the boughs where shadows sway.
The fireflies dance, a gleaming sight,
As dusk unfolds into the night.

The leaves they rustle, secrets told,
Of ancient tales and treasures old.
The breeze that sighs, a tender muse,
Invokes the dreams that we might choose.

With every breath, the twilight sings,
Of hopes and fears, of fragile things.
In every flicker, magic breathes,
The heart finds warmth as daylight leaves.

The stars awake with eager eyes,
Beneath their watch, the world complies.
In shimmering tides, our spirits rise,
To dance on whispers from the skies.

# The Alchemist's Secret Dance

In the stillness of a moonlit night,
An alchemist stirs with pure delight.
Potions bubbling in a silver glass,
Transforming shadows as they pass.

With every twirl, the colors blend,
A symphony where spirits lend.
The dance of elements, wild and free,
Crafting wonders, just to see.

In whispered chants, the secrets weave,
A tapestry of what we believe.
Gold from lead, the myth unbound,
In swirling mists, the truth is found.

The candles flicker, casting light,
On ancient books and arcane flight.
Each step a spell, each breath a chance,
In the alchemist's secret dance.

As dawn approaches, shadows flee,
The world awakens, what shall be?
But in the heart of night, they stay,
The whispers of magic fade away.

# Echoes from the Celestial Veil

Beneath the stars, a silence reigns,
Echoes ripple through time's lanes.
The cosmos hums a haunting tune,
A lullaby beneath the moon.

With every star, a story glows,
Of dreams and fears the heart bestows.
In every twinkle, secrets lie,
Waiting for souls who dare to fly.

The veil of night, a mystic shroud,
Where thoughts take flight and hearts feel proud.
The universe sings with ancient voice,
Guiding the lost to make their choice.

In ethereal realms, the echoes blend,
A gentle breeze, where worlds extend.
Listen closely, the whispers call,
They promise magic to us all.

When light descends, the echoes wane,
Yet in our hearts, they still remain.
A tender trace of what's been known,
In echoes from a veil once shown.

# Spirals of Magic in the Moonlight

In moonlight's grasp, the world transforms,
As magic brews in quiet storms.
With every swirl, the shadows bend,
Creating realms where dreams ascend.

Spirals twist in soft embrace,
Carving paths through time and space.
An ancient rhythm, wild and free,
Invokes the secret of what may be.

The night enfolds with velvet grace,
Invitations to a hidden place.
In dances spun of silver threads,
Ethereal beings weave their spreads.

With twinkling sparks, the air ignites,
Chasing away the fleeting nights.
In each heartbeat, a wish takes flight,
Born from the spirals of the night.

Through glowing trails, the magic flows,
As ebb and flow of starlight glows.
In moonlit dreams, where wonders blend,
The spirals weave, and lives transcend.

# The Ballet of Celestial Whispers

In night's embrace, the stars do gleam,
A dance of dreams, a silken beam.
Whispers float on the cool night air,
As magic twirls with delicate flair.

Moonlight weaves through branches high,
Soft lullabies beneath the sky.
Each note a thread, a story spun,
In twilight's heart, where dreams are won.

The shadows blush in silver light,
Twilight's curtain dims the sight.
Yet here we find the bravest souls,
In whispered waltz, our spirit rolls.

Each twirl reveals a hidden fate,
Through cosmic dance, we gravitate.
With every step, the silence sings,
In harmony, the night softly clings.

And thus beneath the cosmic dome,
Where every star can find a home,
The ballet ends, but dreams remain,
In whispered tones, our hearts sustain.

# Threads of Time and Enchantment

Through the glimmer of the ages past,
A tapestry of moments cast.
With threads of gold and silver spun,
A chronicle of all we've done.

Each stitch a breath, a tale to weave,
In patterns dark and light, we believe.
Time's river flows, a gentle guide,
Through shadowed valleys, we now bide.

In every silence, echoes gleam,
Of laughter shared, of every dream.
The fabric sways in twilight's glow,
In whispers soft, our secrets flow.

Yet falter not, for hope remains,
In every thread, the joy, the pains.
The fabric folds to shape our fate,
In sorrows lost, love we create.

So gather round the cozy fire,
Let stories spark and dreams inspire.
For time's enchantment forever lies,
In hearts entwined beneath the skies.

# The Reverie of Flickering Fantasies


In corners where the shadows creep,
Flickering dreams awaken from sleep.
Whispers flit on the air so light,
In a world where day fades into night.

Mirrors gleam with a mystic touch,
Reflecting hopes we cherish much.
The stars above our secrets hold,
A tapestry of legends bold.

With every flicker, a vision bright,
A chance to dance through realms of light.
Enchantments swirl in colors rare,
A symphony of dreams laid bare.

So lose yourself in this reverie,
Where fantasies waltz, wild and free.
Let shadows guide with their gentle pull,
In the quiet dusk, your heart is full.

Though dawn may break, its golden thread,
Will weave together what dreams have said.
For in this dance, our spirits soar,
In flickers bright, forevermore.

# Journey through the Twisted Essence

In twisted paths where shadows play,
We wander on, both lost and stray.
The essence calls, a siren's song,
In every step, where we belong.

The trees entwined with tales of yore,
Guard secrets whispered, dreams galore.
Each rustling leaf, a message clear,
In nature's breath, we hold so dear.

Though winding roads may cause a tear,
A glimpse of hope will conquer fear.
Through murky depths, the light shines true,
In every darkened twist, find you.

As threads of fate are loosely spun,
From shadows deep, new journeys run.
With every twist, the heart will feel,
In essence pure, we learn to heal.

So take my hand, let's journey deep,
Through twisted times, our visions leap.
In essence rich, we trust the quest,
For in our hearts, we are always blessed.

# Patterns Woven by Celestial Hands

In twilight's embrace, the stars arise,
Their shimmering threads in the vast skies.
Each twinkle a story, a myth untold,
Woven in silence, a tapestry bold.

Glimmers of hope in the dark of night,
Patterns emerge, bathed in silver light.
A dance of the cosmos, a beautiful trance,
In the heart of the heavens, a mystic romance.

Elysian patterns that swirl and splay,
Guide us through shadows where dreams play.
Each constellation whispers a part,
Of secrets that linger in the cosmic heart.

As stardust settles on slumber's brow,
The universe beckons, inviting us now.
With every heartbeat, we feel the pull,
Of patterns and rhythms eternally full.

So, let us gaze up, for time's a mere haze,
In the tapestry woven, we find endless ways.
To connect our own stories with those up above,
In the patterns of starlight, we find endless love.

# Rhythms of the Dream Weaver

Amidst whispered winds, the dream weaver sings,
Crafting soft echoes, with feathery wings.
In the realm of slumber, where shadows hold sway,
A symphony stirs as night greets the day.

Beneath silken skies, visions weave and entwine,
Moments suspended in fabric divine.
Threads of imagination, both fragile and bold,
Spin tales of wonder in colors untold.

Lullabies float on the breath of the night,
Embracing our souls in a tranquil light.
With each rhythmic pulse, our fantasies bloom,
Dancing on dreams, away from the gloom.

As dawn's gentle fingers begin to unfurl,
The dream weaver sighs, weaving the whirl.
Every echo lingers, a spark of delight,
In the heart of the dreams that sparkle so bright.

So rest here awhile, in the warm guiding glow,
Of rhythms that pulse where the night breezes blow.
The dream weaver's magic will softly ignite,
A journey through realms, beyond day and night.

# The Serene Undulations of Night

As shadows deepen, silence takes flight,
The world unwinds in the arms of the night.
A cradle of calm, where whispers abide,
In the serene undulations, our fears start to slide.

Moonbeams glisten on the gentle sea,
Curving and curling, they beckon to me.
A lull of the waves, a breath taking pause,
In the embrace of darkness, we find our cause.

Stars shimmer softly, like sparks in the mist,
Lighting the paths that are oftentimes kissed.
Each twinkling promise a beacon of grace,
Guiding our dreams to a tranquil place.

The night whispers secrets wrapped tightly in sighs,
With floating reflections and lingering goodbyes.
We dance with the echoes, we sway with the light,
In the serene undulations that cradle the night.

So linger, dear heart, in this moment so rare,
Beneath velvet skies where the world seems to care.
In the hush of the evening, let solace be known,
In the gentle undulations, we are never alone.

## Wandering Through Silken Realms

In gardens of mist, where shadows conspire,
We wander through silk, with dreams to inspire.
Each step a whisper, a delicate glide,
In realms of enchantment, where secrets abide.

The moon's silver touch paints the paths we take,
In the heart of the night, as the dreamers awake.
Through whispers of starlight and dewdrop's embrace,
We wander through wonder, discovering grace.

With every soft rustle, the night's gentle breath,
Leads us through journeys where dreams dance with
death.
In the silken embrace of twilight's warm hue,
We find fragments of magic, old and new.

Unfolding like petals, each moment we find,
The tapestry woven in the threads of the mind.
In the heart of the labyrinth, let laughter unfurl,
As we wander through silken, transcendent worlds.

So linger a while in this beautiful sweep,
Let the whispers of night cradle you to sleep.
For wandering through realms of illusion is bliss,
In the tapestry woven, find your own wish.